STATES

NORTH DAKOTA

A MyReportLinks.com Book

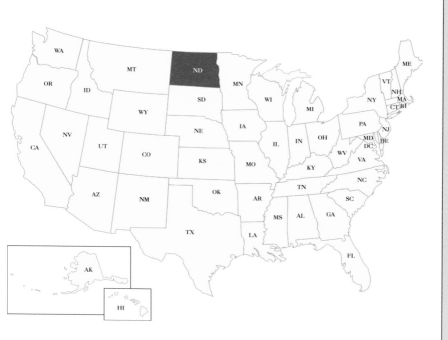

Ron Knapp

MyReportLinks.com Books

an imprint of

 Enslow Publishers, Inc.

Box 398, 40 Industrial Road
Berkeley Heights, NJ 07922
USA

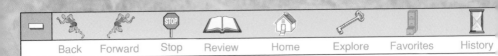

For Phil and Pattie Walter

MyReportLinks.com Books, an imprint of Enslow Publishers, Inc. MyReportLinks is a trademark of Enslow Publishers, Inc.

Copyright © 2003 by Enslow Publishers, Inc.

Library of Congress Cataloging-in-Publication Data

Knapp, Ron.
  North Dakota / Ron Knapp.
    p. cm. — (States)
Summary: Discusses the land and climate, economy, government, and history of the state of North Dakota. Includes Internet links to Web sites. Includes bibliographical references and index.
  ISBN 0-7660-5119-6
  1. North Dakota—Juvenile literature. [1. North Dakota.] I. Title.
II. States (Series : Berkeley Heights, N.J.)
  F636.3.K63 2003
  978.4—dc21
                              2002156365

Printed in the United States of America

10 9 8 7 6 5 4 3 2 1

To Our Readers:
Through the purchase of this book, you and your library gain access to the Report Links that specifically back up this book.
The Publisher will provide access to the Report Links that back up this book and will keep these Report Links up to date on **www.myreportlinks.com** for three years from the book's first publication date.
We have done our best to make sure all Internet addresses in this book were active and appropriate when we went to press. However, the author and the Publisher have no control over, and assume no liability for, the material available on those Internet sites or on other Web sites they may link to.
The usage of the MyReportLinks.com Books Web site is subject to the terms and conditions stated on the Usage Policy Statement on **www.myreportlinks.com**.
In the future, a password may be required to access the Report Links that back up this book. The password is found on the bottom of page 4 of this book.
Any comments or suggestions can be sent by e-mail to comments@myreportlinks.com or to the address on the back cover.

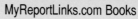
Contents

MyReportLinks.com Books
Great Books, Great Links, Great for Research!

MyReportLinks.com Books present the information you need to learn about your report subject. In addition, they show you where to go on the Internet for more information. The pre-evaluated Report Links that back up this book are kept up to date on **www.myreportlinks.com**. With the purchase of a MyReportLinks.com Books title, you and your library gain access to the Report Links that specifically back up that book. The Report Links save hours of research time and link to dozens—even hundreds—of Web sites, source documents, and photos related to your report topic.

Please see "To Our Readers" on the Copyright page for important information about this book, the MyReportLinks.com Books Web site, and the Report Links that back up this book.

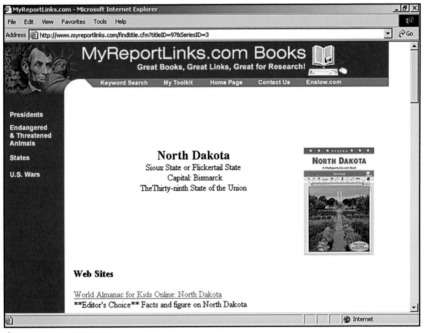

Access:

The Publisher will provide access to the Report Links that back up this book and will try to keep these Report Links up to date on our Web site for three years from the book's first publication date. Please enter **SND1834** if asked for a password.

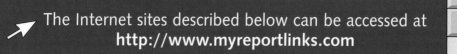

Report Links

The Internet sites described below can be accessed at
http://www.myreportlinks.com

▶ *World Almanac for Kids Online:* **North Dakota** *EDITOR'S CHOICE

The *World Almanac for Kids Online* provides facts and statistics about
land and resources, population, government, economy, and history. You
will also find easy-to-read charts.

Link to this Internet site from http://www.myreportlinks.com

▶ **Lewis & Clark in North Dakota** *EDITOR'S CHOICE

The Lewis & Clark in North Dakota Web site tells the story of Lewis
and Clark's adventures around the country with particular attention
paid to their time spent in North Dakota.

Link to this Internet site from http://www.myreportlinks.com

▶ **Explore the States: North Dakota** *EDITOR'S CHOICE

America's Story from America's Library, a Library of Congress Web site,
tells the story of North Dakota. Here you will learn what the name
"North Dakota" means. You will also find links to other interesting
anecdotes about the state.

Link to this Internet site from http://www.myreportlinks.com

▶ **Today In History: North and South Dakota** *EDITOR'S CHOICE

On November 2, 1889, North and South Dakota were admitted to the
Union. This Web site describes what it was like in the Dakotas at this
time. Learn about the American Indians that inhabited the land, Lewis
and Clark's expeditions, and the Homestead Act.

Link to this Internet site from http://www.myreportlinks.com

▶ **U.S. Census Bureau: North Dakota** *EDITOR'S CHOICE

The U.S. Census Bureau provides quick facts about the state of North
Dakota. Here you will learn about the businesses, geography, and
residents of the state.

Link to this Internet site from http://www.myreportlinks.com

▶ **The Northern Great Plains, 1880–1920** *EDITOR'S CHOICE

North Dakota's history is explored throughout this Web site. Learn
about the state's interesting geography and climate, the American
Indians who inhabited the land, the fur trade, ranching, and about the
state's current industries.

Link to this Internet site from http://www.myreportlinks.com

Report Links

The Internet sites described below can be accessed at
http://www.myreportlinks.com

▶ *Bismarck Tribune:* **Sakakawea and the Fur Traders**

At this Web site you will find a collection of articles related to Sakakawea, the fur traders, and Lewis and Clark.

Link to this Internet site from http://www.myreportlinks.com

▶ **Buffalo-Bison**

The American Bison Web site provides a brief profile of the bison, including information about its physical characteristics, habitat, diet, life span, and other interesting facts.

Link to this Internet site from http://www.myreportlinks.com

▶ **Germans from Russia Heritage Collection**

The North Dakota State University Libraries present the history and culture of German people living in Russia who settled in North Dakota. View photographs of traditional Russian-German foods, and read newspaper articles.

Link to this Internet site from http://www.myreportlinks.com

▶ **Historical Society of North Dakota**

The State Historical Society of North Dakota offers information about Lewis and Clark, Sakakawea, historic sites in North Dakota, and the history of the state.

Link to this Internet site from http://www.myreportlinks.com

▶ **Infoplease: North Dakota**

Infoplease.com provides essential information about the state of North Dakota. Learn about North Dakota's geography, economy, government, and history.

Link to this Internet site from http://www.myreportlinks.com

▶ **KVLY TV: Tower Facts**

Learn interesting facts about the world's tallest man-made structure, located in North Dakota. Find out the total weight of materials used to build the structure, how long it took, and by how many workers. You will also find other interesting trivia facts.

Link to this Internet site from http://www.myreportlinks.com

Report Links

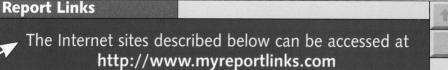

The Internet sites described below can be accessed at
http://www.myreportlinks.com

▶ **Lewis and Clark**

Explore the expeditions of Lewis and Clark at PBS' Lewis & Clark
Web site. Included is information about their exploration of what is
now North Dakota. You can also read the biographies of the members
of the "Corps of Discovery," including Sacagawea.

Link to this Internet site from http://www.myreportlinks.com

▶ **Local Legacies: North Dakota**

Local Legacies, a Library of Congress Web site, describes many of
North Dakota's interesting local legacies, such as the Medora Musical
and Norsk Hostfest.

Link to this Internet site from http://www.myreportlinks.com

▶ **Netstate: North Dakota**

From basic facts to famous people, Netstate provides essential
information about the state of North Dakota. Here you can view
statistics and learn about geographical features of the state.

Link to this Internet site from http://www.myreportlinks.com

▶ **North Dakota Geological Survey**

Lewis and Clark were the first to explore in what is now North
Dakota. Read essays about their explorations, and learn about
paleontology, minerals, and the geology of the state.

Link to this Internet site from http://www.myreportlinks.com

▶ **North Dakota Tourism: Maps**

This site has a list of useful North Dakota maps. There are several to
choose from, including canoeing rivers, forests, and national wildlife
refuges. You will also find historic sites and scenic highway routes.

Link to this Internet site from http://www.myreportlinks.com

▶ **Roadside America: North Dakota**

Here you will find quirky tidbits about North Dakota. View photos
of interesting objects, such as the world's largest historical quilt, the
enchanted highway, and the world's largest buffalo.

Link to this Internet site from http://www.myreportlinks.com

Report Links

→ The Internet sites described below can be accessed at
http://www.myreportlinks.com

▶**Roger Maris**
North Dakota was the home of Roger Maris, a former major-league baseball player who broke Babe Ruth's home run record. This Web site describes his early years, stats and facts, and the Roger Maris Museum, located in Fargo, North Dakota.

Link to this Internet site from http://www.myreportlinks.com

▶**Royal BC Museum**
The Royal British Columbia Museum brings us the history of the ancient weapon, the *atlatl*. View pictures of various pieces as well as drawings that show how the weapon was held and used.

Link to this Internet site from http://www.myreportlinks.com

▶**State of North Dakota—The Office of the Governor**
The State of North Dakota, Office of the Governor Web site holds the biography of Governor John Hoeven and First Lady Mickey L. Hoeven. You will also learn about the governor's initiatives and other issues regarding North Dakota.

Link to this Internet site from http://www.myreportlinks.com

▶**Stateline: North Dakota**
The Stateline.org Web site allows you to compare North Dakota statistics with those of other states. This information covers budget and taxes, crimes and prisons, environment, and income and poverty.

Link to this Internet site from http://www.myreportlinks.com

▶**Stately Knowledge: North Dakota**
Read facts about the State of North Dakota, and view the state flag. See a listing of major industries, points of interest, and bordering states.

Link to this Internet site from http://www.myreportlinks.com

▶**Theodore Roosevelt Association**
President Theodore Roosevelt established many national parks in North Dakota. At the Theodore Roosevelt Association Web site you can learn about these parks as well as explore the life of the former president.

Link to this Internet site from http://www.myreportlinks.com

Any comments? Contact us: **comments@myreportlinks.com**

Report Links

The Internet sites described below can be accessed at
http://www.myreportlinks.com

▶ **Theodore Roosevelt: Bully for North Dakota**
At this Web site you will learn that Theodore Roosevelt attributed his
presidency to his experiences in North Dakota. You will also find
information about Theodore Roosevelt National Park.

Link to this Internet site from http://www.myreportlinks.com

▶ **Theodore Roosevelt National Park**
At the National Park Service Web site you can explore Theodore
Roosevelt National Park. Click on "InDepth" to learn more about the
park's history.

Link to this Internet site from http://www.myreportlinks.com

▶ **Today In History: Laura Ingalls Wilder**
Today In History, a Library of Congress Web site, tells the story of
Laura Ingalls Wilder. The stories she wrote about her family's
experiences were similar to the experiences of other families that
pioneered the northern Great Plains.

Link to this Internet site from http://www.myreportlinks.com

▶ **United Tribes Technical College: History of the North
Dakota Indian Tribes**
Learn the history of the North Dakota Indian tribes. Included is
information on the various tribes, forts, and reservations. You can also read
about the different treaties that were signed with the tribes of the area.

Link to this Internet site from http://www.myreportlinks.com

▶ **U.S. Geological Survey: Programs in North Dakota**
The U.S. Geological Survey Web site provides information about
topographic mapping, geologic mapping, water-resource data, and
other earth science topics.

Link to this Internet site from http://www.myreportlinks.com

▶ **Walking With Dinosaurs: Dino Fact File**
From ABC comes fascinating facts about dinosaurs. Included in this
"Fact File" is information about dinosaurs that once roamed North
Dakota: the Triceratops, Tyrannosaurus, and Deinosuchus.

Link to this Internet site from http://www.myreportlinks.com

North Dakota Facts

▶ **Capital**
Bismarck

▶ **Gained Statehood**
November 2, 1889,
the thirty-ninth state

▶ **Population**
642,200*

▶ **Bird**
Western meadowlark

▶ **Tree**
American elm

▶ **Song**
"North Dakota Hymn" (words
by James W. Foley and music by
Dr. C. S. Putnam)

▶ **Fish**
Northern pike

▶ **Beverage**
Milk

▶ **Fossil**
Teredo petrified wood

▶ **Grass**
Western wheatgrass

▶ **Dance**
Square dance

▶ **Motto**
Liberty and Union, Now and
Forever: One and Inseparable

▶ **Nicknames**
Peace Garden State; Flickertail
State; Roughrider State; Land of
the Dakotas

▶ **Flag**
A dark-blue flag. In the middle is
a bald eagle holding an olive
branch in one claw and a bundle
of arrows in the other. The eagle
carries in its beak a ribbon say-
ing "*E Pluribus Unum*" ("One
nation made up of many states").
Across its chest is a shield with
thirteen stars representing the
original thirteen states. Just
above the eagle's head is a gold
fan-shaped design, representing
the birth of a new nation, the
United States. Below the eagle is
a red scroll that has "North
Dakota" written across it.

Population reflects the 2000 census.

10

A Land of Giants

Sixty-five million years ago, giants roamed North Dakota. It was the perfect place for big animals. Most of the area was covered by water. Trees, bushes, and flowers surrounded the sea. It was warm and wet. There was plenty to eat—even for the giant, plant-eating triceratops. The huge dinosaur needed lots of food. Adults grew to be nine feet tall and almost thirty feet long. They weighed up to fourteen thousand pounds. Its name "triceratops" means "three-horned face," and that is what it had. One horn pointed down from between its eyes. Two over the eyes pointed up and out. Behind them was a bony frill to protect the neck.

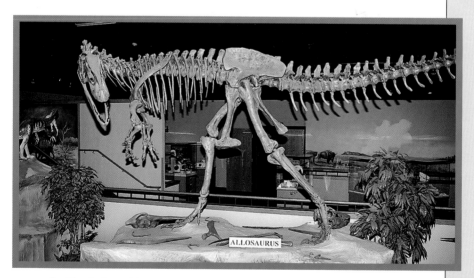

▲ The Dakota Dinosaur Museum, located in Dickinson, North Dakota, contains twelve replicated dinosaur skeletons and one full-scale, real triceratops skeleton.

An even bigger giant living in North Dakota was the tyrannosaurus, one of the largest meat-eaters ever to walk the earth. It usually walked upright on its hind legs. The tyrannosaurus had a huge head with a jaw that was full of sharp teeth.

As big and fierce as it was, even a tyrannosaurus had to be careful. Sitting quietly in the shallow North Dakota waters was a giant crocodile called deinosuchus. It looked a lot like today's crocodiles—except that it was four times as big.

Today the sea is gone, the weather has cooled, and the era of the dinosaurs is over. That does not mean there are no giants left in North Dakota. In fact, there are even a few dinosaurs left. A full-scale model of a triceratops guards the entrance to the Dakota Dinosaur Museum in Dickinson. Inside is the real thing—or what is left of one—the reassembled skeleton of a triceratops.

One of the world's finest tyrannosaurus skeletons was discovered in the North Dakota Badlands. Parts of it are on display in Bowman at the Pioneer Trails Regional Museum. A complete skeleton of a triceratops is there as well.

▶ Interesting Statues

North Dakota also has a few more modern giants. One of the world's biggest cows stands near New Salem. It is thirty-eight feet tall and fifty feet long, and made of fiberglass. The giant cow was built as a tribute to the state's dairy farmers. Local residents have nicknamed it Salem Sue.

Just outside Jamestown is the world's biggest bison. It may be the only one made of concrete. It weighs 120,000 pounds, standing 26-feet high and 46-feet long. The giant buffalo was erected at the National Buffalo Museum and Visitor Center. Millions of buffaloes once grazed the plains of North Dakota and neighboring states until they were almost hunted to extinction. Thanks, in part, to many North Dakota ranches, the buffalo has made a comeback. Visitors can watch a herd graze near the museum located in Jamestown.

A giant animal statue in Bottineau is not quite as serious. Tommy Turtle, all thirty-three feet of him, stands at the foot of the Turtle Mountains. In honor of the area's most popular winter sport, he is riding a snowmobile. Turtle Lake, North Dakota, is the site of the annual United States Turtle Racing Championship.

Near the state capitol building in Bismarck is a smaller sculpture of a real-life person who was a giant of history. A twelve-foot statue of Sacagawea pays tribute to one of the United States' most famous women. She was a Shoshone Indian who served as a guide and translator for the Lewis and Clark Expedition almost two hundred years ago.

△ The National Buffalo Museum is committed to preserving the history of the American bison. Included in its many displays is the world's largest bison.

Of course, not everything big in North Dakota is a statue. Garrison Dam in the middle of the state is the fifth-largest earthen dam in the world. The 2.5 mile long structure crossing the Missouri River has created giant Lake Sakakawea (another way to spell Sacagawea). It is the third-largest reservoir in the country. The lake covers more than 368,000 acres and is 178 miles long.

Lake Sakakawea supplies water to thousands of residents and businesses. By regulating its flow, Garrison Dam helps prevent the river from flooding. Using the stream of water passing through it, the dam also produces vast amounts of electricity.

The KVLY-TV tower is another real giant. In fact, it is one of the tallest man-made structures in the world. The tower was erected outside Blanchard, North Dakota, in 1963. Stack the Eiffel Tower on top of the Washington Monument, then put them both on top of the Great Pyramid at Giza, and they would not be as tall as the tower. At 2,063 feet, it is more than 800 feet higher than the Empire State Building. Its signal can reach television viewers in thirty-five counties in North Dakota and Minnesota.

North Dakotans are also proud of their capitol building. While most state capitols have just a few stories under a dome, the North Dakota building stretches nineteen stories. It has earned the nickname "skyscraper of the prairie."

The giant sunflower is one of the world's biggest flowers—and North Dakota grows more of them than any other state. Some of the plants grow taller than ten feet. The heads, or blossoms, can measure more than a foot across. A big one can have more than one thousand seeds. Sunflower seeds are a popular snack food, but they are also used to produce vegetable oil.

No talk of giant North Dakotan food should go without mentioning a tasty "bite" that was entered into the *Guinness Book of World Records.* In 1982, the people of Rutland created the world's largest hamburger. It took almost ten thousand people to eat the 3,591-pound burger.

As attractive as a giant hamburger may be, most of the attractions that bring visitors to the state emphasize its wild, natural beauty or the efforts of the earliest settlers to make a home.

▷ Theodore Roosevelt National Park

Teddy Roosevelt was one of thousands of adventurous Americans who fell in love with the Dakota Badlands in the nineteenth century. More than 70,000 acres of that land has been preserved in the Theodore Roosevelt National Park. The park is divided into two main sections, the North Unit near Watford City and the South Unit near Medora.

Over the centuries, the Little Missouri River has carved the soft rock of the Badlands into canyons and cliffs. Small, craggy hills stretch beautifully across the horizon. Not just grays and browns. Thousands of years of erosion have exposed red, yellow, and even blue rock.

Theodore Roosevelt National ▷ Park maintains a herd of 70 to 110 wild horses by auctioning off surplus horses every few years. Prior to 1970, the National Park Service tried to get rid of all the wild horses, however this policy was reversed when these animals were recognized as part of the historical setting.

Here and there, erosion has exposed black stretches of a soft coal called lignite. Lightning sometimes ignites the coal. If it starts burning, the lignite can smolder for decades. The fire bakes the surrounding sand and rock, turning it to a hard material called scoria that resembles brick.

Different kinds of tough grasses grow around the various rock formations. In the summer, bright wildflowers dot the landscape. The plants provide food and protection for a wide variety of animals.

Millions of little prairie dogs live in groups among the grass. They provide food for other animals such as coyotes and badgers. Theodore Roosevelt National Park is also home to porcupines, bobcats, beavers, wild horses, deer, and rabbits. The park has more than 170 species of birds, including the golden eagle.

Miles of trails meander through the park. Long stretches of road provide scenic drives. Park rangers give talks and conduct nature walks. Usually, campgrounds are crowded all summer long. In the winter, skiers and snow-mobiles take over the area.

Roosevelt's first ranch house, called the Maltese Cross Cabin, has been relocated and renovated in the South Unit. The site of Roosevelt's Elkhorn Ranch is also part of the park. To get to the Elkhorn Ranch, visitors have to travel a dirt road for twenty miles before fording a small river. There is nothing left of the ranch except the foundation of the main building.

▷ What It Was Like to Be a Pioneer

Fort Mandan, Lewis and Clark's winter headquarters from 1804 to 1805, has been reconstructed near Washburn. Costumed guides are on hand to explain their mission.

The nearby North Dakota Lewis and Clark Interpretive Center has artifacts and paintings.

There are eleven buildings, including a schoolhouse and a church, at the Dale and Martha Hawk Museum near Wolford. Exhibits include items from homestead days as well as antique autos.

Pioneer Village, located near Kenmare, has eighteen old buildings, including a post office, bank, and windmill.

Icelandic State Park, located near Cavalier, features exhibits about the state's first settlers from Iceland. Its Pioneer Heritage Center has a church, barn, homestead, and community hall. The same park also hosts the Gunlogson Homestead.

The Prairie Village Museum, with twenty-seven restored buildings, is located in Rugby. It is close to a small cairn, or pile of rocks, that marks the exact geographical center of the North American continent. The people of Rugby were so proud of that distinction that they also built the Geographical Center Museum.

The largest preserved village in North Dakota is Bonanzaville, USA, located in West Fargo. There are forty

▲ The Lewis and Clark Interpretive Center is located in Washburn, North Dakota.

buildings, including a log cabin, jail, town hall, train depot, and general store. It even has a mansion used by one of the bonanza farmers. American Indian artifacts are included in a museum. Bonanzaville also has antique tractors, airplanes, and automobiles.

▶ Forts From the Old Days

Early in the nineteenth century, Fort Union was the center of the fur trade for most of Dakota. Some of its structures have been rebuilt, and it has been designated a national

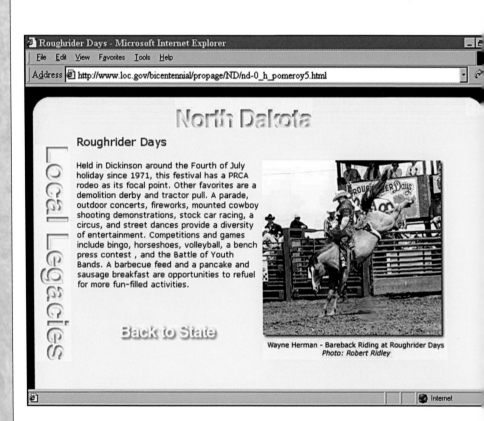

Roughrider Days - Microsoft Internet Explorer

File   Edit   View   Favorites   Tools   Help

Address http://www.loc.gov/bicentennial/propage/ND/nd-0_h_pomeroy5.html

North Dakota

Local Legacies

Roughrider Days

Held in Dickinson around the Fourth of July holiday since 1971, this festival has a PRCA rodeo as its focal point. Other favorites are a demolition derby and tractor pull. A parade, outdoor concerts, fireworks, mounted cowboy shooting demonstrations, stock car racing, a circus, and street dances provide a diversity of entertainment. Competitions and games include bingo, horseshoes, volleyball, a bench press contest , and the Battle of Youth Bands. A barbecue feed and a pancake and sausage breakfast are opportunities to refuel for more fun-filled activities.

Back to State

Wayne Herman - Bareback Riding at Roughrider Days
Photo: Robert Ridley

Internet

▲ *Each year the Roughrider Days is held in Dickinson, North Dakota, to celebrate the state's western culture. A PRCA rodeo is the main feature supported by many other activities, including a demolition derby and tractor pull.*

historic site. Many of its exhibits concentrate on the furs that brought the earliest white men to North Dakota.

The guardhouse at Fort Abercrombie is original. The stockade and other buildings have been rebuilt.

Fort Totten State Historic Site, located near Devils Lake, houses one of the country's best-preserved forts from the pioneer days. Sixteen of its buildings, including the hospital, commissary, and American Indian boarding school, are original.

Fort Abraham Lincoln State Park is the site of the post from which Lieutenant Colonel George Custer led his men to disaster at the Battle of the Little Bighorn in 1876. The cavalry and infantry buildings have been reconstructed. There is also a museum that focuses on nineteenth-century life, including American Indians, soldiers, railroads, and homesteading.

The site was used by the Mandan Indians for more than two hundred years, beginning around 1575. They did not abandon it until just before the Lewis and Clark Expedition.

▶ Museums

The North Dakota Heritage Center, located near the state capitol in Bismarck, houses exhibits, archives, and a research library.

More recent history is the focus of the Dakota Buttes Museum, located in Hettinger. Besides many military items donated by local veterans, it also houses a recreated dentist's office as well as a hairdressing salon.

Dickinson's Dakota Dinosaur Museum, Pioneer Museum, Joachim Regional Museum, and Pioneer Machinery Museum tell the story of North Dakota from the time of the dinosaurs to the present.

Fort Abraham Lincoln State Park preserves the cavalry and infantry post that Lt. George Armstrong Custer and his troops rode out from to fight the Battle of Little Bighorn. The park also contains a campground and an American Indian village on the premises.

▶ Seeing the Animals

North Dakota's most famous animal is the buffalo. Herds of buffalo can be seen in Theodore Roosevelt National Park. Another herd is penned next to an observation deck at the National Buffalo Museum and Visitor Center in Jamestown.

North Dakota is on a central flyway, or sky trail, used every spring and fall by millions of migrating birds. Several national wildlife refuges have been set aside for the birds— Audubon (near Garrison); Des Lacs and Lostwood (near Kenmare); J. Clark Salyer (near Minot); Kelly's Slough (in Emerado); Lake Ilo (near Dickinson); Long Lake (near Moffit); and Tewaukon (near Cayuga). The refuges are wonderful places to watch the migrating birds. Some hunting is also allowed.

Millions of fish get their start at the Garrison Dam National Fish Hatchery. Eggs spawned by pike, bass, chinook salmon, and wild pallid sturgeon are hatched there. In the fall, visitors can watch salmon swimming up a fish ladder.

The Valley City National Fish Hatchery produces bass, perch, muskie, walleye, bluegill, and catfish.

The Dakota Zoo, located in Bismarck, contains native animals such as bison and bobcats, but also more than one hundred other species of animals from around the world.

International Peace Garden

Canada and the United States have the longest unfortified border in the world. To celebrate the friendship of the two countries, the beautiful International Peace Garden was planted along the border north of Dunseith, North Dakota. It covers 888 acres in the United States and 1,451 in Canada.

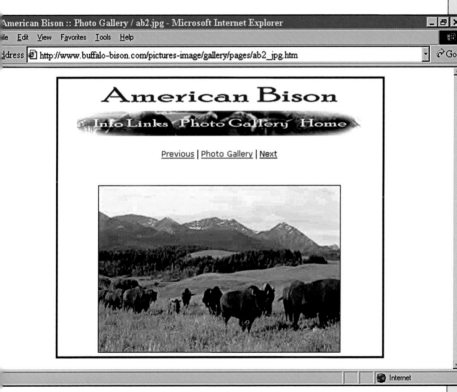

American Bison :: Photo Gallery / ab2.jpg - Microsoft Internet Explorer

File Edit View Favorites Tools Help

Address http://www.buffalo-bison.com/pictures-image/gallery/pages/ab2_jpg.htm

The American Bison is the largest mammal in North America. By 1830, most of the plains herds had been killed off due to westward expansion. While it is estimated that 30 million to 70 million bison once roamed North America prior to European settlement, only about 65,000 existed by 2000.

▲ *The International Peace Garden is located on the border of North Dakota and Manitoba, Canada. The peace tower (shown above) is the garden's focal point. It was built in the early 1980s to celebrate the garden's fiftieth anniversary.*

Visitors may walk, bike, or drive through 150,000 flowers planted every summer. A round garden is always planted in the shape of a clock. Instead of numbers the flowers are planted to form the face of the clock. An underground motor moves the big white hands, making it a giant working clock.

A Peace Chapel, Peace Tower, and Carillon Bell Tower have been built on the grounds. There are facilities for camping and picnicking. Organized camps for young athletes and musicians are held there every year.

▷ International Golf

Friendly Canadian-American relations are celebrated in a different way at a unique golf course built between Portal, North Dakota, and North Portal, Saskatchewan, Canada.

Golfers sign up to play at the Gateway Cities Golf Club clubhouse, which stands in the United States. Then they cross a gravel road into Canada where they play the first eight holes. After teeing off on the ninth hole in Canada, they cross the border again and sink the ball in the cup in the United States.

Land and Climate

Almost from the time it was first settled, the area in the northern plains has been known as Dakota. The word comes from one of the American Indian tribes that lived there when white settlers arrived.

The area was called the Dakota Territory when it was first organized. North Dakota and South Dakota kept the name when they became states in 1889.

▶ The North Dakotans

European immigrants have stopped coming in large numbers to North Dakota. The days of homesteading are over, so most of the people who live in the state are descendants of the immigrants who moved there a century ago.

▲ Lake Metigoshe, nestled in the Turtle Mountains, is one of the most popular vacation spots in North Dakota.

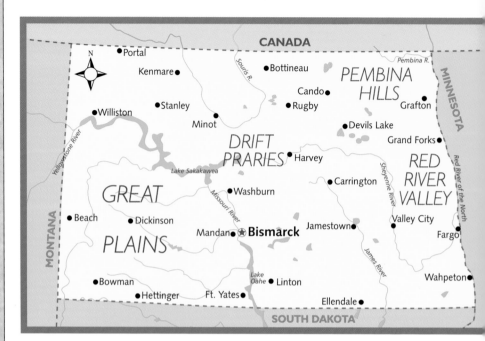

▲ *A map of North Dakota.*

According to the 2000 U.S. Census, just over 92 percent of all North Dakotans are white. The biggest minority group is American Indian, with 4.9 percent of the residents. The Hispanic-American population is 1.2 percent. African Americans make up only .6 percent of the total.

▶ The Land

North Dakota has three main geographic regions. The Red River Valley is a thin strip of land located along the eastern border with Minnesota. The soil is particularly rich, so many farms are located there. This region has the most people.

The Pembina Hills separate the Red River Valley from the Drift Prairie, which takes up most of the middle of the state. There are some hills and a few valleys, but the Drift Prairie is mostly a flat area. In the north are the Turtle Mountains. There are many small lakes.

The Great Plains stretch from Canada down across North Dakota, all the way to Texas. The region covers the southwestern half of the state. It is a flat area with few hills. The Badlands, hills of sandstone, shale, and clay, are here. Much of the land is used to graze cattle.

Streams and rivers in most of the state drain into the Missouri River which flows from Montana to Missouri, flowing through North Dakota. The James River, in the Drift Prairie, flows south. The Red River of the North, in the east, flows north into Canada and Hudson Bay.

The land of North Dakota has changed little since white settlers began arriving three centuries ago. Most of the state is empty. It is possible to drive the lonely highways for hours without passing another vehicle.

Not everything about North Dakota, though, is big. People there are also proud of some very low numbers. In 2000, of all fifty states, North Dakota had the lowest overall crime rate. It also had the lowest violent crime rate and the fewest robberies and murders. Residents brag that North Dakota is the safest state.

In 1997, the Children's Rights Council named North Dakota as the best state to raise children. It based the rating on the low crime levels and several other factors. Fewer North Dakota marriages end in divorce than in most other states, and its schools have a high graduation rate.

Most North Dakotans are pleased that their state is one of the least crowded. Its biggest city is Fargo, with only about 90,599 residents. Just three other cities, Minot, Grand Forks, and Bismarck, have more than thirty thousand.

Almost half of North Dakota's 642,200 people live on farms, in rural areas, or in small towns. In fact, farms or ranches cover more than 90 percent of the state's land.

Since 1930, the population of the United States has more than doubled from 122,775,046 to 281,421,906. That is an increase of almost 229 percent. During the same time, North Dakota's population has fallen from 680,845 to 642,200, a decrease of more than 5 percent.

▶ The Climate

Because North Dakota has no tall mountains, winds blow freely across the state, and the weather can change quickly. Usually, the northern part of the state is a few degrees cooler than the southern part.

Because humidity is almost always low, summers are usually sunny and warm, but pleasant. Average temperatures in July range from 67°F to 73°F.

Winters can be bitterly cold. January average temperatures range from 3°F to 14°F. The nasty winds sweeping across the plains usually make it feel even colder. Annual snowfall averages about 32 inches.

Different areas of the state get between 13 and 20 inches of rain a year.

Famous North Dakotans

In 2000, the U.S. Treasury Department issued a golden dollar coin. There are two people pictured on the coin—Sacagawea and her son, Pomp. Both of them have strong ties to North Dakota.

▶ Sacagawea and Pomp

Sacagawea was a Shoshone Indian girl, who lived with her family near the Knife River. In 1800, when she was only about twelve years old, her village was invaded by a war

▲ Lake Sakakawea is named after Sacagawea, the Shoshone woman who helped Lewis and Clark along their expedition. With a surface area of approximately 138,000 acres and 178 miles in length, the lake is the largest man-made reservoir in the United States.

party of Hidatsa Indians, and Sacagawea was kidnapped and forced to live at Fort Mandan. Later, she married Toussaint Charbonneau, a French trader. Together they joined the Lewis and Clark Expedition.

Bringing Sacagawea along on their expedition was probably the luckiest thing Lewis and Clark ever did. When they were hungry, she knew how to find foods such as artichokes and wild beans. When a boat almost tipped over during a terrible storm, Sacagawea saved the medicine, paper, and books that were almost washed away. When the travelers needed horses and supplies, Sacagawea begged a group of Shoshone to help them. By a lucky coincidence, the leader of the Shoshone was a brother she had not seen since her kidnapping. He traded them everything they needed in exchange, mainly, for some horses.

Just having Sacagawea and her son along made the expedition safer. The American Indian tribes of the area did not feel threatened by a group that included a woman and her baby.

After the expedition was over, Clark praised Sacagawea in a letter to her husband. "Your woman who accompanied you that long dangerous and fatiguing rout to the Pacific Ocean and back deserved a greater reward for her attention and services. . . . than we had in our power to give her."[1]

Her son, Jean Baptiste Charbonneau, was born on February 11, 1805, while the group waited for the winter to end at Fort Mandan. When the snow melted, Sacagawea carried him on a cradle board. William Clark nicknamed the boy Pomp.

When he was just six years old, Jean Baptiste moved to present-day St. Louis, Missouri, to live with Clark. In 1823, he traveled to Europe with a German prince. When he finally returned to the United States as an adult, he became a mountain man and a fur trader.

Historians are not sure what happened to Sacagawea. Some sources report that she died a few years after the expedition ended. Others believe she lived to be one hundred years old on a Shoshone reservation in Wyoming.

Lawrence Welk

A few decades ago, Lawrence Welk was one of the most popular and successful television stars in the country.

The son of German-speaking immigrants from Russia, Welk was born on March 11, 1903, in a sod farmhouse in Strasburg. He wrote, "My earliest clear memory is crawling toward my father who was holding his accordion. I can still

▲ *This painting, "Lewis and Clark on Columbia," by Frederic Remington depicts Sacagawea, with Pomp on her back, standing in the background behind Meriwether Lewis, William Clark, and Touissant Charbonneau.*

recall the wonder and delight I felt when he let me press my fingers on the keys and squeeze out a few wavering notes."[2]

When Welk was seventeen years old, he made a deal with his father. If his father would buy him a $400 accordion, he would work on the family farm for four more years. On his twenty-first birthday, Welk and his accordion left North Dakota. Soon he had his own band. Over the years, Welk added more and more musicians until he conducted his own orchestra in the 1930s.

One of his shows was broadcast on a television station in Los Angeles. Many felt the program should have been a flop because Welk spoke with a heavy German accent and did not play music that was popular on the radio. His favorite comment after most numbers was "Wunnerful, wunnerful." The orchestra specialized in bubbly, happy tunes. He called it "champagne music." His trademark was bubbles floating through the air. For more than twenty years, his television show remained popular, especially with older viewers.

Peggy Lee

Norma Delores Egstrom was born in Jamestown on May 26, 1920. Her mother died when she was four years old, and she had a miserable childhood. When her father was too drunk to work, Norma walked to the nearby railroad depot and did his job.

Because of her distinctive husky, but smooth voice, Egstrom was able to sing on area radio programs. A station manager in Fargo gave her a new, easier-to-remember name—Peggy Lee. She moved to Chicago, and in 1941, she became the lead singer for Benny Goodman's band.

▲ *Peggy Lee poses at the Grammy Awards ceremony held on February 24, 1982.*

Soon she was recording popular songs. "Fever" and "Is That All There Is?" were two of her biggest hits. Her recording and performing career lasted more than fifty years.

Lee is best known to children for the part she played in making *Lady and the Tramp,* Walt Disney's classic animated movie. She helped write many of the songs and provided the voices for several of the characters, including Peg and the Siamese cats. Lee died on January 21, 2002.

▶ Roger Maris

Roger Maris was a star athlete at Fargo High School. He was so good, in fact, that the University of Oklahoma, one

of the best college teams in the country, recruited him to play football. Instead, Maris decided to play baseball. He signed a $15,000-contract with the Cleveland Indians in 1953.

After four years in the minor leagues, Maris joined the Indians as an outfielder in 1957. After a season and a half in Cleveland, Maris was traded to the Kansas City Athletics, then to the New York Yankees.

In 1961, Maris was locked in a home-run battle with his friend and teammate, Mickey Mantle, to break the single-season total of 60, set in 1927 by Babe Ruth.

Maris was in an awkward position. Some fans did not want to see the record broken, because Ruth was the most popular athlete who had ever played the game. Almost everybody who wanted to see the record broken seemed to be cheering for Mantle, who was by far the most popular Yankee.

Maris did not enjoy the fans rooting against him. "They acted as though I was doing something wrong, poisoning the record books or something," he said.[3]

After Mantle was injured, Maris had the home-run race to himself. On the last day of the season, he broke Ruth's record by blasting his sixty-first home run of the year.

◀ *Roger Maris.*

Tools   Search   Notes   Discuss   Go!

Maris died in 1985. In 1998, when Mark McGwire broke his record by hitting his sixty-second home run, Maris's grown children were guests of honor in the stands in St. Louis. His career is honored at the Roger Maris Baseball Museum, in his hometown of Fargo, North Dakota.

Warren Christopher

In 1925, Warren Christopher was born in Scranton, North Dakota. He attended college and law school in California before becoming a clerk for U.S. Supreme Court Justice William O. Douglas.

Christopher served as deputy attorney general when Lyndon B. Johnson was president. Then, under President Jimmy Carter, Christopher became deputy secretary of state. He negotiated the release of American hostages from Iran and helped normalize relations with China. He also helped win ratification of the treaty that returned the Panama Canal to Panama.

In 1993, President Bill Clinton appointed Christopher secretary of state. During his four years in the post, he traveled more than 780,000 miles, representing the United States around the world. When he retired in 1997, President Clinton said, "The cause of peace and freedom and decency have never had a more tireless or tenacious advocate."[4]

Phil Jackson

As a basketball player and a coach, Phil Jackson has earned more championship rings than he has fingers. Jackson was a star basketball player at Williston High School. In college, he averaged 27.4 points per game as a senior at the University of North Dakota and earned All-America honors.

In 1967, Jackson was drafted by the New York Knicks of the National Basketball Association (NBA). While he

played for the team, they won two NBA titles. A few years after retiring as a player, he was hired to coach Michael Jordan and the Chicago Bulls.

Many people thought Jackson was a strange coach. He seldom yelled at his players. Instead, when they played poorly, he quietly clipped his fingernails on the bench. He asked his players to read books to make them think.

Jackson's approach worked. In his nine years with Chicago, the team won six NBA championships. He and Jordan left the Bulls after the 1997–98 season. After taking a year off, Jackson became head coach of the Los Angeles Lakers. Then, with the big center Shaquille O'Neal leading the way, the Lakers won titles in 2000, 2001, and 2002.

Government and Economy

North Dakota's governor is elected to a four-year term. There are other statewide offices. These include attorney general, treasurer, secretary of state, and superintendent of public instruction.

North Dakota still uses the same constitution its citizens adopted in 1889. Laws are written by the Legislative Assembly, which is composed of the Senate and House of Representatives. Being a legislator is not a full-time job. The Legislative Assembly meets only eighty days every two years.

Legislators meet and work in the "Skyscraper of the Prairie," the tall state capitol building located in Bismarck.

There are five judges on the state's highest court, the Supreme Court. The state also has county and district courts.

Most of North Dakota's revenue comes from a sales tax and an extraction tax paid on petroleum produced in the state.

▶ Jobs

Throughout its history, most North Dakotans have relied on wheat production and cattle ranches for jobs. Unfortunately, because of the use of modern farm machinery, there are fewer agricultural jobs than in the past.

For almost the entire twentieth century, the state's citizens struggled to find jobs. Many North Dakotans have given up the effort and left the state to seek work elsewhere. That is why the state's population was lower in 2000 than it was in 1930.

In the last couple decades of the twentieth century, energy resources provided some new jobs. A huge oil field was discovered in the western part of the state. Natural-gas wells were put in operation, mainly in the northwest. Energy companies also began to mine lignite coal, mostly in the Badlands. Many people also work in journalism and mass media. North Dakota has roughly a hundred newspapers, sixty radio stations, and twenty television stations.

▲ *After the first capitol building was destroyed by fire in 1930, the second and current state capitol building was completed four years later. Due to the economic hardship at this time, much of the decorations planned for the building had to be removed.*

History

Long after the dinosaurs died out, much of North America was covered by a number of huge glaciers. When the ice melted about ten thousand years ago, mammoths and giant bison roamed the plains.

Many scientists believe that people known as Paleo-Indians followed the animals across a land bridge that once connected Asia to North America. There were plenty of mammoth and bison in North Dakota.

Small groups of the new settlers followed the wild herds. They killed the animals with a clever weapon called an *atlatl*. It was a flexible dart that was thrown with a quick, whiplike motion of a throwing stick. The atlatl was fast and deadly. It also allowed the hunters to stay a safe distance from their prey.

To supplement the meat in their diet, some of the Paleo-Indians gathered wild food that grew in the plains. Over the years, some of them became farmers. Corn was the crop they grew best. They built lodges out of logs and brush. A new weapon, the bow and arrow, replaced the atlatl. By then, the mammoth and giant bison were extinct. The modern buffalo was hunted instead.

▶ The Whites Come

For centuries, the Plains Indians enjoyed little interference in their way of life.

In 1610, the English were the first to claim part of North Dakota. When Henry Hudson explored Hudson

Hidatsa Indians

In 1804, travelling northwest from the Mandan village of Rooptahee, it was a short trip to Mahawha, the first of three villages of the neighboring Hidatsas. The Hidatsas, allies of the Mandans, inhabited a stretch of the Knife River in what later became central North Dakota. Along with the Mandans, they formed the hub of trade in the Upper Missouri region, attracting a wide variety of Indian and European traders each fall.

Hidatsa villages were designed in a fashion similar to their Mandan counterparts. Earth lodges were clustered irregularly around a central plaza, and were occupied for approximately 7 to 12 years. A log wall surrounded the village to protect it from invaders. Mahawha was located at the meeting of the Knife and Missouri rivers, and was home to about 50 warriors. The next village to the north, Metaharta, had about 50 lodges, but the northernmost village, Menetarra, was the

Internet

> ▲ The Hidatsa Indians were one of nearly fifty American Indian tribes that Lewis and Clark came into contact with along their expedition across the West. The Hidatsa inhabited a stretch of the Knife River located in what is now central North Dakota.

Bay, he said all the land with rivers that drained into the bay belonged to England. That included eastern North Dakota.

After his own exploration, René-Robert Cavelier, Sieur de La Salle, then claimed all the land with rivers that drained into the Mississippi River for France. That included another chunk of North Dakota.

The first white Europeans arrived in North Dakota in 1738. Pierre Gaultier de Varennes, Sieur de La Vérendrye, was a French Canadian looking for a long river that would flow from the middle of North America to the "Western

Sea," or Pacific Ocean. He traveled as far as the Missouri River, but he never found a water route to the Pacific.

Fur Trading

French fur traders followed Vérendrye. Buffalo hides and furs from other animals were popular in Europe. Fortunes could be made supplying the demand. The French did not have to do all the killing themselves. Instead, they got most of their furs from the American Indians by trading them beads, cloth, muskets, or pieces of metal.

By the time the fur traders arrived, there were two main types of American Indians in North Dakota. The Assiniboine, Cheyenne, Chippewa, Lakota, and Dakota were nomads with no permanent villages. They relied on the buffalo for food. Wherever the herds went, the tribes followed.

The other group, the Mandan, Hidatsa, and Arikara, did not have to move. They lived in small villages made up of earth lodges along the Missouri River. Their villages were surrounded by huge gardens; they did not always have to hunt for food.

Alexander Henry the Younger, was a trader who built a post to trade with the American Indians. After a few other whites came to live there, it became North Dakota's first permanent home for European settlers. They named it Pembina.

Lewis and Clark

When France sold Louisiana to the United States in 1803, it was a great bargain for Americans. Most of North Dakota was included in the sale. President Thomas Jefferson wanted a thorough description of the new land. He ordered Meriwether Lewis and William Clark to conduct a "voyage of discovery" up the Missouri River.

Lewis and Clark left St. Louis with a crew of about fifty men on May 14, 1804. By October, they were in North Dakota. They decided to stop for the winter near villages of the Mandan and Hidatsa Indians. They called their settlement Fort Mandan. The long journey helped open North Dakota and the rest of the Louisiana Purchase to American settlement.

The Border

For a few years, Great Britain and the United States argued about the border between North Dakota and Canada. The Convention of 1818 settled the problem. The border would eventually be a line stretching hundreds of miles along the northern boundaries of Washington, Idaho, Montana, North Dakota, and Minnesota. This is known as the 49th parallel.

The American Indians are Forced Out

A series of American forts were built throughout North Dakota to protect white settlers and to watch the American Indians. The native peoples were angry that they were losing their land—and their way of life.

Lieutenant Colonel George Custer led about 260 men from Fort Abraham Lincoln, near Bismarck, to one of the most disastrous defeats in American military history. Custer and his troops were wiped out by Sioux, Cheyenne, and Arapaho warriors led by Crazy Horse and Sitting Bull at the Battle of the Little Bighorn, which actually took place in present-day Montana in 1876.

It was a rare victory for American Indians. After a few battles, the United States troops controlled the Plains. The American Indian tribes retreated to Canada or surrendered and moved to reservations.

▶ A Great Deal

Congress set up the Dakota Territory in 1861. It included all the land that would one day become both North and South Dakota as well as sections of Montana and Wyoming. Yet the new territory was a long way from the established states, and at first, few settlers wanted to come there.

Congress passed the Federal Homestead Law in 1862. That meant settlers could get 160 acres of free land. All they had to do was live on it and plant crops or improve the land. This encouraged many Americans to move west.

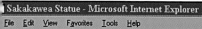

Sakakawea Statue - Microsoft Internet Explorer

File   Edit   View   Favorites   Tools   Help

Address ⌨ http://www.state.nd.us/hist/StatueHist.htm   ⌐ Go

History of Sakakawea Statue on State Capitol Grounds, Bismarck

A 12-foot-high bronze statue of Sakakawea and her baby son, Baptiste, stands at the entrance to the North Dakota Heritage Center on the state capitol grounds in Bismarck. The statue, by Chicago artist Leonard Crunelle, depicts Sakakawea with her baby strapped to her back, looking westward toward the country she helped to open.

Mink Woman, a Hidatsa Indian from the Fort Berthold Indian Reservation in North Dakota, served as a model for the statue. A painting by Margarethe E. Heisser of Minneapolis, now in the collections of the State Historical Society of North Dakota, shows Mink Woman dressed in a buckskin dress. This image was used by Crunelle to create a small model of the Sakakawea statue.

Crunelle was born in Pas de Calais, France in 1872. He emigrated to Brazil, Indiana, in 1882, then to Decatur, Illinois a few years later. He worked in the mines of Decatur until 1893, when he went to Chicago as a student and apprentice of famed sculptor Lozado Taft. In addition to the Sakakawea statue, his commissioned works also include fountains for Grant Park; the Oglesby Memorial in Chicago's Lincoln Park; the Logan Monument at Vicksburg, Mississippi; and a portion of Lincoln's Tomb in Springfield, Illinois. Crunelle died in Chicago in 1944, at the age of 72.

🌐 Internet

▲ *Sakakawea, also known as Sacagawea, was a Shoshone Indian woman that guided Lewis and Clark in their exploration of the West. This 12-foot bronze statue of Sakakawea and her newly born son, Jean Baptiste, faces west. It is located in Bismarck at the North Dakota Heritage Center.*

By 1872, the Northern Pacific Railway had reached North Dakota. Towns such as Fargo and Bismarck grew because they were along its route. The trains made it easy for settlers to come to the new territory. More than 100,000 people came to North Dakota between 1879 and 1886.

Bonanza Farms

Not all of the farms were small ones run by single families. A few corporations and rich speculators bought thousands of acres to raise just one crop—wheat. They used newly-invented machinery for planting and harvesting. They also took advantage of the latest scientific research on farming.

http://memory.loc.gov/award/ndfa/ndfahult/c200/c243r.jpg - Microsoft Internet Explorer

File   Edit   View   Favorites   Tools   Help

Address   http://memory.loc.gov/award/ndfa/ndfahult/c200/c243r.jpg

Done   Internet

▲ Families such as this one came west in the 1800s by way of covered wagon. Those who waited until the early 1900s were able to travel on the Great Northern Railroad.

The huge farms were successful, earning their owners thousands of dollars. They became known as "bonanza" farms. The definition of a bonanza is a lucky, profitable enterprise, so that was a very appropriate name.

The Beef Boom

A few North Dakotans hoped that cattle would make them as rich as wheat had made the bonanza farmers. They thought that the Badlands along the Little Missouri River would be a perfect spot to graze cattle. Badlands are areas where water has eroded the land, so the land has little use. However, these areas are good for grazing. There are plenty of streams for water and good grass for food.

Unfortunately for the cattle ranchers, the winter of 1886–87 was brutal. Long months of snow and freezing temperatures killed most of their cattle.

Theodore Roosevelt, for one, enjoyed ranching. He said, "I never would have been president if it had not been for my experiences in North Dakota."[1]

Immigrants Come

Despite the bad luck of the ranchers, new citizens continued to arrive in the Dakota Territory. Many of the people who were homesteading land were not yet Americans. They were immigrants from Europe. Most of them were from Norway and the other Scandinavian countries. Thousands of Germans that had been living in the Ukraine also left for a new life in America. Plenty still came from the eastern United States, as well.

Bismarck, the city that would become the state capital, was named in honor of Otto von Bismarck, the man who made Germany a unified nation in 1871.

Between 1890 and 1920, the state's population skyrocketed from 190,983 to 646,872. By 1915, more than 79 percent of the population were either immigrants or the children of immigrants.

▶ Statehood

As their population grew, the people of the Dakota Territory began to think about becoming several states. They believed the territory was just too big to become one state. Congress agreed. It portioned off the territory to Montana and Wyoming and divided the rest into two rectangular-shaped

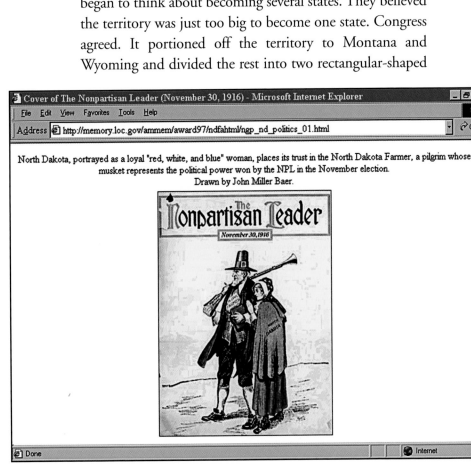

The cover of The Nonpartisan Leader portrays North Dakota as a loyal companion to the farmer. In 1915, North Dakota farmers formed the Nonpartisan League, a political party that believed there should be state ownership of banks, grain elevators, and flour mills.

states—North Dakota and South Dakota. Both joined the Union on November 2, 1889. Which joined first? Nobody knows. President Benjamin Harrison shuffled their admission papers without looking before signing them. Even he did not know which state was first. Since North Dakota is first alphabetically, it gets credit for being the thirty-ninth state. South Dakota is the fortieth.

Farmers Come Together

In its early days as a state, North Dakota had few banks, flour mills, or grain elevators. To use such services, farmers had to go to Minnesota.

In 1915, thousands of farmers formed the Nonpartisan League, which called for the state itself to set up banks and other businesses. Soon the league was a powerful political force. The North Dakota state government established a bank and a mill.

Trouble on the Farms

The 1930s were a terrible time for North Dakota. A severe drought limited crops, and the Great Depression that was plaguing the country caused few people to have enough money to live decently.

It took about ten years for the state to recover. Then, in the late 1940s, farm prices fell, and many farmers went bankrupt. Workers left North Dakota to find jobs elsewhere.

In the late 1950s, the state established a commission to help attract new industry. The 1960s saw the U.S. Air Force open military bases in the state that helped boost the economy. Oil wells brought income to people in the 1970s. More recently, the state has relied on its agricultural industry, while still looking to attract more business to the Peace Garden state.

Chapter 3. Famous North Dakotans

1. William Clark, "18. Nearing Home: August 17, 1806," *Discovering Lewis and Clark*, 1998, <http://www.lewis-clark.org/journal_aug17-1806.htm> (December 18, 2002).

2. Lawrence Welk, quoted in Jo Ann Winistorfer, "Lawrence Welk: 'uh-one and uh-two . . .'," *North Dakota Living*, May 2002, p. 30.

3. Roger Maris, quoted in USA Today, "Roger Maris: A season for the ages," *USA Today Baseball*, 1998, <http://www.usatoday.com/sports/baseball/marisbio.htm> (December 18, 2002).

4. Bill Clinton, as quoted by North Dakota Information Technology Department, "Theodore Roosevelt Rough Rider Award: Warren Christopher 1925– ," *State of North Dakota Office of the Governor*, 2002, <http://www.governor.state.nd.us/awards/rr-gallery/christopher.html> (December 18, 2002).

Chapter 5. History

1. Theodore Roosevelt, as quoted by North Dakota Tourism, "Theodore Roosevelt: Bully for North Dakota!" *Attractions in the West*, 1998, <http://www.ndtourism.com/regions/west/WestRoosevelt.html> (December 18, 2002).

Further Reading

Edwards, Judith. *Lewis and Clark's Journey of Discovery in American History.* Berkeley Heights, NJ: Enslow Publishers, 1999.

Fradin, Dennis Brindell. *North Dakota.* Danbury, Conn.: Children's Press, 1998.

Gaines, Ann Graham. *The Louisiana Purchase in American History.* Berkeley Heights, NJ: Enslow Publishers, Inc., 2000.

Hintz, Martin. *North Dakota.* Danbury, Conn.: Children's Press, 2000.

Kummer, Patricia K. *North Dakota.* Minnetonka, Minn.: Capstone Press, Incorporated, 2003.

McDaniel, Melissa. *North Dakota.* Tarrytown, NY: Marshall Cavendish Corporation, 2001.

Morgan, Kathleen O'Leary. *North Dakota in Perspective 2002.* Lawrence, Kans.: Morgan Quitno Corporation, 2002.

Sanford, William R., and Carol R. Green. *Sacagawea: Native American Hero.* Berkeley Heights, NJ: Enslow Publishers, Inc., 1997.

Schueler, Donald G. *Theodore Roosevelt: A MyReportLinks.com Book.* Berkeley Heights, NJ: Enslow Publishers, Inc., 2002.

Thompson, Kathleen. *North Dakota.* Austin, Tex.: Raintree Steck-Vaughn Publishers, 1996.